Did Y...

EDIN...

A MISCELLANY

Compiled by Julia Skinner

With particular reference to the work of Clive Hardy

THE FRANCIS FRITH COLLECTION

www.francisfrith.com

Based on a book first published in the United Kingdom in 2005 by The Francis Frith Collection®

This edition published exclusively for Identity Books in 2009 ISBN 978-1-84589-412-2

British Library Cataloguing in Publication Data

Did You Know? Edinburgh - A Miscellany
Compiled by Julia Skinner
With particular reference to the work of Clive Hardy

The Francis Frith Collection
Frith's Barn, Teffont,
Salisbury, Wiltshire SP3 5QP
Tel: +44 (0) 1722 716 376
Email: info@francisfrith.co.uk
www.francisfrith.com

Printed and bound in Singapore

Front Cover: **EDINBURGH, JOHN KNOX'S HOUSE 1897** 39125p

The colour-tinting is for illustrative purposes only, and is not intended to be historically accurate

AS WITH ANY HISTORICAL DATABASE, THE FRANCIS FRITH ARCHIVE IS CONSTANTLY BEING CORRECTED AND IMPROVED, AND THE PUBLISHERS WOULD WELCOME INFORMATION ON OMISSIONS OR INACCURACIES

CONTENTS

INTRODUCTION

The lively modern city of Edinburgh stands on historic foundations.
By the beginning of the 7th century the site occupied by Edinburgh
Castle was a stronghold of the Gododdin, but in 638 it fell to the
Northumbrians, at that time the most powerful of the Anglo-Saxon
kingdoms, whose territory stretched from the Forth to the Humber
and to the south of the Mersey. The name of Edinburgh is thought to
derive from 'Edwin's burgh', as Edwin was an early 7th-century king of
Northumbria.

Edinburgh has had a turbulent history, and has often been taken
by the English and won back by Scottish forces. Some protection for
the castle was gained by the building of the King's Wall in 1450. After
Scotland's defeat by the English at Flodden in 1513 another wall, the
Flodden Wall, was built around Edinburgh, encompassing a wider
area than the King's Wall, which shaped the confines of the city for
around the next 250 years. Unwilling to build outside the safety of
the walls, Edinburgh citizens built upwards, resulting in the 'Lands', or
tenements, sometimes as many as 14 storeys high, giving Edinburgh
a high-rise appearance that made it unique in Europe. The nickname
for Edinburgh, 'Auld Reekie', came about because the city appeared
to be capped by a cloud of 'reek' or smoke. In the late 18th and early
19th centuries new prosperity came to Edinburgh, and development
took place outside the old protective walls. This 'Golden Age' of
Edinburgh was when its magnificent Georgian architecture was built,
making Edinburgh a city of gracious squares, broad thoroughfares
and impressive public buildings, all within a setting enhanced by
public gardens and dominated by its historic castle.

Edinburgh has been home to many names in history, both famous and infamous; great thinkers, scientists, writers, artists, engineers, churchmen and criminals have all walked these streets. Edinburgh's story is full of fascinating characters and events, of which this book can only provide a brief glimpse.

EDINBURGH, HOLYROODHOUSE PALACE AND ARTHUR'S SEAT 1897 39168

EDINBURGH PHRASES

On Edinburgh friendliness:

'I'll chum yi' - I'll go with you, keep you company.

Edinburgh people are considered mean by Glaswegians, or 'weegies', who make the following comparison between Edinburgh and Glaswegian hospitality:

The Edinburgh greeting - ***'Come on in, you'll have had your tea'.***

The Glasgow greeting - ***'Come on in, and have a bite to eat'.***

On Edinburgh's climate:

' The delicate die early, and I, as a survivor, among bleak winds and plumping rain, have sometimes been tempted to envy them their fate.' (Robert Louis Stevenson)

Some part of the surface painted area of the 135 acres of the Forth Bridge is always being repainted, so the proverbial expression ***'painting the Forth Bridge',*** used to describe an endless task, is based on fact.

HAUNTED EDINBURGH

The ruins of Old Woodhouselee, a mansion to the south of Edinburgh, are said to be haunted by the ghost of Lady Hamilton, who was banished into the freezing winter night without any clothing after the castle was seized by the Regent Moray. She froze to death, and her naked ghost is said to haunt the area, sometimes holding the body of a dead child (Lady Hamilton was pregnant at the time of her eviction). When the ghost has been seen in winter, there are never any footprints in the snow.

> It is no surprise that Mary, Queen of Scots, her husband Lord Darnley and her murdered secretary Rizzio are said to haunt Holyroodhouse Palace, but a more unusual ghost is that of Bald Agnes, who appears, naked, in the garden. Apparently Agnes was stripped and tortured on suspicion of her being a witch in 1592.

A phantom drummer who is sometimes heard at Edinburgh Castle is said to warn of bad news.

> The Devil is said to drive a coach drawn by headless horses up Lawnmarket and into the Bow; his disciple Major Weir sits inside the coach. Major Weir, who had the care of the Marquess of Montrose before his execution, announced to the astounded Edinburgh citizens in 1670 that he had committed incest with his sister from the age of 16 to the age of 50, fornication with the maid for 20 years, and bestiality with his horses and cows. He was tried and found guilty on all charges, and was strangled before his body was burnt at the stake, but the fact that he also admitted to being a warlock appears to have been ignored.

A building in Buckingham Terrace is said to be haunted by a sea-captain, who killed himself after murdering a baby whilst he was drunk.

EDINBURGH MISCELLANY

In Old Greyfriars', Edinburgh:

> Here snug in grave my wife doth lie!
> Now she's at rest, and so am I.

On the grave of Catherine Smith, who beguiled a mean and ageing Scotsman out of his wealth, in Edinburgh:

> When Miss Smith was twenty
> She had lovers in plenty;
> When Miss Smith got older
> Her lovers got colder;
> Then came Serjeant Spankie
> And Miss Smith said thankie.

On a tomb in St George's Church, Edinburgh:

> Stranger, tread this ground with gravity,
> Dentist Brown is filling his last cavity.

In 1341 Edinburgh Castle was in English hands, occupied by the troops of Edward III, under the command of Guy, Count of Namur. The Scots used a cunning plan to win back the castle: William of Douglas disguised himself and his men as merchants bringing supplies to the garrison. They dropped their loads so that the gates could not be closed; then they held on fighting until joined by the main force, whereupon they took back the castle. Of the English garrison of 49 men-at-arms, 60 archers and six watchmen, most were butchered, and their bodies were flung over the walls onto the crags where they were left to rot.

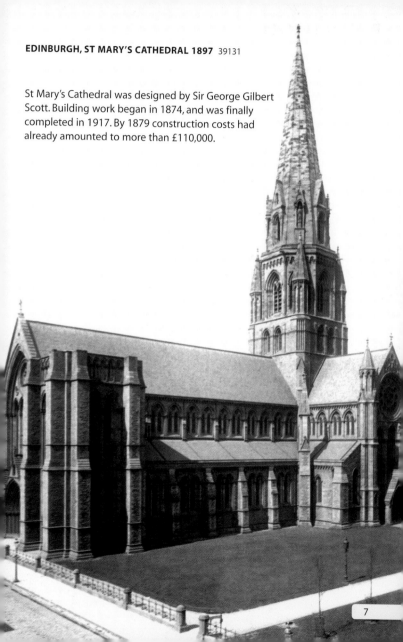

EDINBURGH, ST MARY'S CATHEDRAL 1897 39131

St Mary's Cathedral was designed by Sir George Gilbert Scott. Building work began in 1874, and was finally completed in 1917. By 1879 construction costs had already amounted to more than £110,000.

EDINBURGH, THE CASTLE FROM THE GRASSMARKET 1897 39121

The photograph above gives an idea of the imposing bulk of the great Half-Moon Battery, the parapet of which was added in the 1690s. Behind the battery are the Palace and the Great Hall. On this side of the castle are most of the buildings constructed before 1625 which have survived above ground level in a recognisable form. Each weekday at 1pm a cannon is fired from the Half-Moon Battery on Edinburgh Castle as a time check, a tradition which began in 1861.

Edinburgh Castle was one of the most advanced castles of its time; many of the natural features of the site were incorporated into the plan to make the best possible use of them. However, when the English King Edward I, 'Longshanks', besieged the castle in 1296 he deployed giant catapults to batter the garrison into submission, and succeeded in obtaining their surrender after three days and nights of rock-dodging.

Edinburgh Castle became the principal residence of Malcolm III and his wife Queen Margaret. The earliest surviving structure, Queen Margaret's Chapel, dates partly from c1100. When Robert the Bruce captured Edinburgh Castle from the English in 1313 he gave orders that this chapel should be left unharmed, although all else was destroyed to prevent the English making military use of the castle in the future. The castle that we see today is, with a few additions, that built by the Earl of Morton following the siege of 1572. Norton succeeded Lennox as Regent, and took the fortress in the name of the infant James VI from the supporters of Mary, Queen of Scots. It was Morton who added the great Half-Moon Battery to the castle's defences.

EDINBURGH, ST GILES' CATHEDRAL 1897 39126

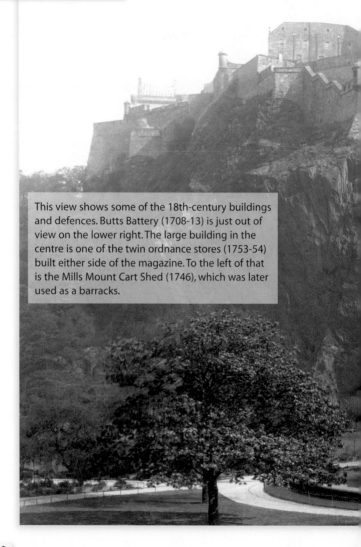

This view shows some of the 18th-century buildings and defences. Butts Battery (1708-13) is just out of view on the lower right. The large building in the centre is one of the twin ordnance stores (1753-54) built either side of the magazine. To the left of that is the Mills Mount Cart Shed (1746), which was later used as a barracks.

**EDINBURGH CASTLE,
FROM PRINCES STREET GARDENS 1897**
39119

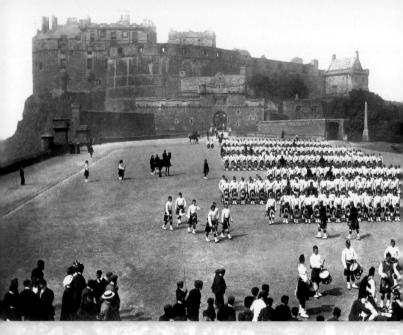

EDINBURGH, BLACK WATCH ON THE CASTLE ESPLANADE 1897 39121a

The Esplanade-cum-parade ground of Edinburgh Castle was laid out in its present form in the 1820s. Of the castle buildings, on the left of the photograph above is the Palace (reconstructed 1617), the Half-Moon Battery and Forewall Battery. The small tower on the right with the angled roof is the Portcullis Gate, the upper part of which was added in 1886-87. In this photograph a battalion of the Black Watch parade on the castle esplanade. Raised by General Wade in 1725, the Black Watch was formerly constituted as a regiment of the line in 1739, and its strength was increased from four to ten companies.

Edinburgh was well served by its tramway system for 85 years; services came to an end in November 1956.

Although Bonnie Prince Charlie managed to occupy Edinburgh in 1745, he failed to capture its fortress, which was held by forces loyal to the Hanoverian King George II.

James III commissioned the construction of 'Mons Meg', a brute of a weapon for its time that made a great hole in James's defence budget as well as anything it was fired at. Deploying Meg was a logistical nightmare: when James IV ordered it to be dragged to the siege of Norham Castle in 1497, it took over 220 men and 90 horses to get it there. In 1680 the cannon burst when it fired a royal salute to Charles II.

EDINBURGH, THE CASTLE, 'MONS MEG' c1950 E24001

Even today Edinburgh Castle looks impregnable. However, an inherent weakness in the defences was the lack of water. The fortress is perched high on a cliff of carboniferous basalt, and the main well is 89 feet deep. Though supplies under normal conditions were adequate, excessive demand during periods of dry weather would lead to it drying up. Following the capture of the castle in 1313, Robert the Bruce ordered it to be slighted so as to render it of no further military use to the English. The well was filled in, and its location was lost until 1381.

James Graham, 5th Marquess of Montrose, was one of the greatest tacticians of the Civil War. Fighting for Charles I, Montrose won victory after victory, often against overwhelming odds. His luck finally ran out at Philliphaugh in September 1645. Returning from the Continent to raise an army in support of Charles I, he was betrayed to the Covenanters and was hanged, drawn and quartered at Edinburgh on 21 May 1650.

The Duke of Gordon held the castle for James VII (James II of England) during the Long Siege of 1689 by the forces of William of Orange. Gordon surrendered the castle on 13 June 1689 owing to sickness and acute shortages of food and water. During 1988-91 excavations unearthed the remains of some of the garrison from this siege. None of the skeletons showed signs of wounds, but all appeared to have died from disease.

In 1645 Edinburgh was struck by a particularly devastating attack of the plague. In Mary King's Close, off the High Street, not one inhabitant survived. The close, little changed, is now part of the City Chambers.

**EDINBURGH, ST GILES' CATHEDRAL,
THE TOMB OF THE MARQUESS OF MONTROSE 1897** 39130

EDINBURGH, FROM THE CASTLE 1897 39101

The waters of Nor' Loch once flowed over the area now occupied by Princes Street Gardens, the railway and Princes Street, and together with an area of marshland formed a part of the castle and the old town's defences. The photograph above gives an indication of the size of the loch. However, this loch and marshland inhibited Edinburgh's expansion. The decision was taken in the 1770s to drain it to allow the development of the new town.

During the Reformation the interior of St Giles' Church was defaced, and the altar and relics were destroyed. In 1559 John Knox was appointed minister of St Giles'. The building was in fact divided into four separate churches, and remained so until the 19th century.

Edinburgh University was founded by James VI in 1582. By the early years of the 20th century the university had 3,000 students, 40 professors, 43 lecturers and 44 examiners.

Begun by William Wallace, principal mason to the Crown in 1628, and completed by William Aitoun, Heriot's Hospital (below) is designed on the courtyard plan with a turreted tower house at each corner. The hospital was founded by George Heriot, goldsmith and banker to James VI. Heriot was immortalised as Jingling Geordie in Sir Walter Scott's 'The Fortunes of Nigel'.
The hospital was not fully completed until 1693, when it saw service as a military hospital.

EDINBURGH, HERIOT'S HOSPITAL 1897 39135

The Canongate was where the canons of Holyrood Abbey entered the Old Town. The tolbooth, with its projecting clock, is one of the most famous landmarks on the Royal Mile. It was built at the end

EDINBURGH, THE CANONGATE TOLBOOTH 1897 39124a

of the 16th century and had a varied career, having been used as a courthouse and a prison. The poles seen here sticking out of the windows of the building in the distance were used for drying washing.

Did You Know?

EDINBURGH

A MISCELLANY

EDINBURGH
THE SCOTT MONUMENT 1897
39112

The Scott Monument was designed by George Kemp and completed in 1844. There are 287 steps to the top. During his lifetime Scott lived at several addresses in the city, the most famous being 39 Castle Street, where he wrote many of the 'Waverley' novels.

The abbey at Holyrood was founded in 1128 for the Augustinian canons by David I, in thanks (and penitence) for being spared when he was attacked by a stag whilst out hunting on a holy day. The chapel at Holyroodhouse Palace is the burial place of David II, James II and James V, and has been described as one of the finest examples of ecclesiastical architecture in Scotland. The chapel was sacked during the conflict of 1688-89 between the forces of James VII (James II) and William of Orange, and even more damage to the chapel occurred in 1768 when the roof fell in.

The Grassmarket was the site of many an execution and the location of the lynching of Captain Porteous following the Porteous Riots in 1736. Captain 'Black Jock' Porteous was appointed captain of one of the companies employed to keep the peace in Edinburgh. At a riot following the execution of Andrew Wilson for smuggling, Porteous ordered his men to fire on the crowd. He was later taken into custody, tried and condemned to death, but because of the circumstances of the case a stay of execution was granted until the king returned from Hanover. There were many people in Edinburgh who hated Porteous; fearing that he would be pardoned, on 7 September a mob broke into the Old Tolbooth, the 'Heart of Midlothian', and hanged him in the Grassmarket. Despite the offering of a large reward for information, no one was ever charged with Porteous's murder.

Work on Holyroodhouse Palace began in about 1500, during the reign of James IV, when the north-west tower was built up against the nave of Holyrood Abbey. Building continued under James V, who added a new tower and quadrangle. The palace was badly damaged when it was set on fire in 1544 by English troops under the Earl of Hertford.

Edinburgh became Scotland's capital in 1437, when James II decided to hold his parliament in the town. Parliament House, in Parliament Square, was where the Scottish government agreed to the Act of Union with England in 1707; according to an old song, the members were 'bought and sold for English gold'.

King Charles II ordered extensive alterations to Holyrood. Between 1670 and 1679 the quadrangle was remodelled in the French style to the designs of Sir William Bruce, the King's Surveyor in Scotland. The strong French influence in Sir William's design reflected the king's passion for all things Gallic.

EDINBURGH, HOPE STREET 1897 39114

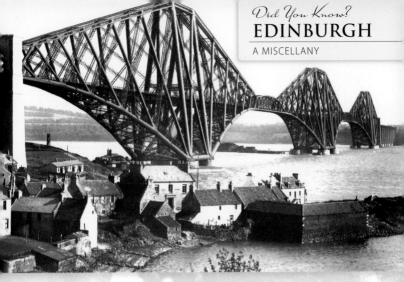

THE FORTH RAILWAY BRIDGE 1897 39145

The Forth Railway Bridge, not far from Edinburgh, was built between 1882 and 1890, and was constructed to carry the North British Railway's main line between Edinburgh and Aberdeen. It is over 2,760 yards long, including approach viaducts, and the tracks run across the bridge 150 feet above sea level. The steel towers stand 360 feet high, and are supported on granite piers; the deepest foundations are 88 feet below high water. The bridge was designed by Sir John Fowler and Sir Benjamin Baker, and cost £3 million to build. Of the workforce of 4,500 men, 57 were killed in work-related accidents.

Donaldson's Hospital in Edinburgh was erected and endowed for the maintenance and education of up to 300 children, of whom 100 had speech and/or hearing difficulties. The benefactor was a wealthy printer who had died in 1880, leaving £200,000 for the project.

EDINBURGH, JOHN KNOX'S HOUSE 1897 39125

The photograph above shows the lower reach of the High Street, looking towards Canongate. The building immediately behind the lamp standard is known as John Knox's house. Dating from the 16th century, the house is said to have been built by the goldsmith of Mary, Queen of Scots. Just how long Knox lived there is open to debate.

The site of the execution of the Marquess of Montrose was at the Mercat Cross in the High Street. Having been declared a traitor in 1644, Montrose was not given the benefit of a trial. After hanging for three hours, his body was taken down and quartered. His head was set upon the tolbooth, and his limbs were sent for public display on the gates of Stirling, Glasgow, Perth and Aberdeen. In 1661 Montrose was allowed a state burial.

The National Gallery of Scotland opened in 1859. The collection included paintings of the Spanish and Italian Schools, and the British were represented by artists such as Gainsborough.

In the background on Calton Hill in the photograph below stands the unfinished monument to the Scottish dead of the Napoleonic Wars, Charles Cockerell's Parthenon. The monument was started in 1822, but the money ran out and it was never completed.

EDINBURGH, WATERLOO PLACE AND THE GENERAL POST OFFICE 1897 39117

Founded in 1823, the Museum of Antiquities, at the foot of
The Mound, housed a statue gallery at one time. There was also
a collection of casts that was only open to art students.

EDINBURGH, THE MUSEUM OF ANTIQUITIES 1897 39115

EDINBURGH, FROM CALTON HILL 1897 39103A

In the foreground of the photograph on page 28 is the castellated bulk of the prison. The old Calton burial ground beyond is where the philosopher David Hume is buried.

> *Within this circular idea*
> *Called vulgarly a tomb,*
> *The ideas and impressions lie*
> *That constituted Hume.*

Much of the Old Town of Edinburgh was rebuilt in the middle of the 16th century following a major fire, but even then it remained notoriously cramped and insanitary. The only way for the inhabitants to get rid of their refuse and empty their chamber pots was by throwing their rubbish into the street at night, for refuse men to shovel it up and cart it away. On Dr Johnson's first visit to Edinburgh in 1773 he is said to have met Boswell in the High Street with the words 'Sir, I smell you in the dark'.

The oldest parish church in Edinburgh, St Giles' was erected in the early 12th century on the site of an older building. In 1385 much of the church was badly damaged by fire, and the rebuilding was not completed until 1460. The tower, which dates from c1495, is topped off with what is considered to be the finest example of a crown steeple in the whole of Scotland. In 1634 Charles I attempted to re-establish the Scottish Episcopal Church, and St Giles' was for a short period elevated to the status of a cathedral. It became a cathedral again under Charles II, only to revert to being a parish church in 1688. The High Kirk of Edinburgh, it is usually referred to as St Giles' Cathedral.

In 1314 Edinburgh Castle was in English hands, held by Peres Lebaud, Edward II's Sheriff of Edinburgh. It was recaptured for the Scots by Thomas Randolph, Earl of Moray. An assault force led by William Francis made their way along an old track up the north precipice, scaled the walls, opened the gates and let in the main Scottish force.

Edinburgh in the early 19th century was the crime scene of the notorious William Burke and William Hare, who both came to Scotland from Ireland, originally as navvies on the Union Canal. At this period the modern science of surgery was still in its infancy, and there was a chronic shortage of bodies for anatomy students to dissect as part of their surgical training. This was the era of the body snatchers, who stole newly buried bodies from graveyards to sell to the anatomy schools. Burke and Hare are often described as body snatchers, but this is erroneous, and in fact their crimes were far worse, since they murdered for profit. Hare had inherited a lodging house in the West Port area of Edinburgh by marrying the landlady when the landlord died, and Burke and his common-law wife Helen MacDougal took rooms there. When one of the other lodgers died owing rent, Burke suggested that they should sell his body to the anatomist Dr Knox to be dissected and used for anatomy instruction. Before long they were murdering people for the express purpose of selling the bodies to the surgeons. It is believed that at least sixteen people were murdered and their bodies sold to the anatomists, for an average of £10 per body. When their crimes were detected, Hare informed on Burke and was eventually set free; Helen MacDougal and Mrs Hare, who had evidently been accessories to the crime if not more fully implicated, also managed to receive acquittals. Burke was executed and publicly dissected on 28 January 1829.

EDINBURGH, ST MARY'S CATHEDRAL 1897 39132

EDINBURGH, WATERLOO PLACE 1897 39116

On the left of the photograph above is the Register House containing the Scottish archives. The statue is of the Duke of Wellington.

Holyroodhouse Palace was the home of Mary, Queen of Scots from 1561 to 1567. It was here that her friend and secretary David Rizzio was murdered by a gang of nobles led by her husband. The pregnant queen was held at swordpoint by the Earl of Ruthven whilst Rizzio was stabbed to death in front of her. It was also at Holyrood that Mary's son James VI of Scotland learned that he had become James I of England. James was the chosen heir of the childless Elizabeth Tudor, and when she died a messenger rode the 400 miles from Richmond, Surrey, to Edinburgh to bring the news; the journey took 62 hours.

One of the most famous stories of Edinburgh is that of Greyfriars' Bobby, a small terrier whose statue is on a fountain near Greyfriars' Church. Bobby's owner was Jock Gray, a shepherd who died in 1858 and was buried in Greyfriars' churchyard; his little dog guarded his grave for the rest of his life. The people of Edinburgh adopted him and made sure he was regularly fed, and when Bobby died in 1872 he was buried beside his master.

Not far from Edinburgh is Roslin, whose chapel is famous for its 'Prentice Pillar' of entwined ribbands. The story is that the chief stonemason went to Italy to study a similar pillar. While he was away, his apprentice worked out how to construct the pillar after having a dream, and built it. When the stonemason returned, he was so jealous of his apprentice's work that he struck the boy dead. On the chapel walls are sculptured heads of the mason, the boy and his weeping mother.

ROSLIN, THE CHAPEL, THE INTERIOR 1897 39164a

In the Palace Yard of Edinburgh Castle is the Scottish National War Memorial, unveiled in 1927. This commemorates the 100,000 Scots who died in the First World War. The memorial depicts, in bronze and

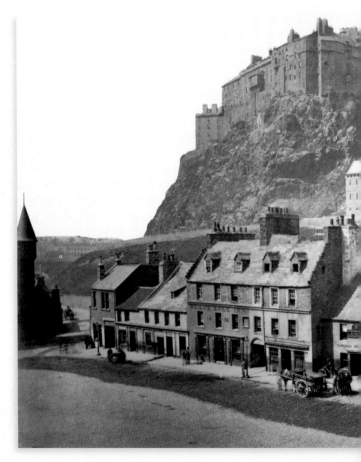

stained glass, every type of war service imaginable, including the contribution of the transport mules, carrier pigeons, and even the mice and canaries used to detect gas in the mines and trenches.

EDINBURGH, THE CASTLE FROM THE GRASSMARKET 1883 E24303

EDINBURGH, THE MUSEUM AND THE CASTLE c1900 E24509

In Canongate churchyard is a gravestone marked 'Clarinda'.
Her real name was Mrs Agnes Maclehose, and she was one of the
great loves of Robert Burns, inspiring the lines:

> 'Had we never lov'd sae kindly
> Had we never lov'd sae blindly,
> Never met - or never parted,
> We had ne'er been broken-hearted…'

In Queen Mary's bedroom at Holyroodhouse Palace are two embroidered
panels which were worked by Mary, Queen of Scots during her long
years of exile and captivity in England, before her execution in 1587 for
involvement in Catholic plots against Elizabeth Tudor. One of the panels
shows a ginger cat, which may represent Elizabeth, gazing at a small
mouse, which may represent Mary herself.

At the turn of the 20th century Princes Street boasted a number of hotels. The most expensive to stay at was the North British at Waverley Station. Next on the list were the Caledonian, the Station and the Royal, followed by the somewhat cheaper Royal British, the Douglas and the Bedford. There was also the Old Waverley, which was a temperance establishment.

At intervals in Canongate the letter 'S' can be seen let into the road. These mark the old sanctuary line of Holyrood Abbey. Once debtors were across that line they could not be apprehended, a right that survived until 1880. Passers-by would watch debtors being chased down the Canongate, and bet on the result.

EDINBURGH, THE UNIVERSITY 1897 39134

The site of the old 'Heart of Midlothian' prison is marked by a heart-shaped pattern on the pavement near St Giles' Cathedral.

EDINBURGH, THE NATIONAL GALLERY 1897 39106

SPORTING EDINBURGH

Heart of Midlothian Football Club once received a world-record fee for one of their star players, Percy Dawson, who was sold to Blackburn Rovers in 1914 for £2,500. The fee went towards part of the cost of a new stand.

Hibernian Football Club led the way into European football. In 1955 the club was invited to enter the new European Champions Cup, thus becoming the first British team to play in European competition. The first match was against the German side Rott-Weiss Essen, with Hibernian winning 4-0 in Germany. They went on to reach the semi-finals, where they lost to the French side, Rheims.

Eric Liddell, one of the most celebrated Olympic athletes ever, was a graduate of Edinburgh University. Liddell was a fine all-round sportsman, but his greatest talent was in sprinting, and especially the 100 metres. He competed in the 1924 Olympics in Paris but did not run in the 100 metres, as the heats were to be run on a Sunday. As a devout Christian, he was not prepared to compete on Sundays. Instead, he entered the 400 metres, and won in a world record time. Liddell's story was made famous in the 1981 film 'Chariots of Fire'.

At the outbreak of the First World War in 1914 the entire playing staff of Heart of Midlothian Football Club decided to sign up for active service, providing a lead for thousands of their supporters to follow. They were the first British team to sign up, many of the players joining 'C' Company of the 16th Royal Scots. Seven players died in the war, and few of the survivors played again for the club. Their lead and sacrifice has not been forgotten, as there is a war memorial to the club at Haymarket, and a remembrance service is held there each year.

QUIZ QUESTIONS

Answers on page 48.

1. What is one of the more complimentary names by which Edinburgh is sometimes known?

2. What was the 'Rough Wooing'?

3. How did the areas known as Upper Bow and Netherbow get their names?

4. Which Edinburgh 'first' can be found in Thistle Court?

5. How did King George IV raise a few Edinburgh eyebrows in 1822?

6. How did Princes Street get its name?

7. Which Edinburgh worthy is believed to have inspired Robert Louis Stevenson's 'Dr Jekyll and Mr Hyde'?

8. Which world-famous philosopher lived in Riddle's Court in Edinburgh and is buried in the old Calton burial ground?

9. From 1778 Adam Smith (1723-90) lived in Edinburgh as commissioner of the Scottish customs. Which revolutionary work of economic theory did he write?

10. What was the traditional cry of warning that Edinburgh people called when they emptied their chamberpots out of windows into the streets?

RECIPE

EDINBURGH ROCK

Ingredients:

1lb (450g) sugar

Pinch of cream of tartar

Half a pint (300ml) water

Flavouring (ie lemon, vanilla, raspberry, ginger or orange) and food colouring of choice

Put the sugar in a heavy saucepan with the water. Bring to the boil and add the cream of tartar. Continue boiling without stirring until a little dropped-in cold water forms a hard lump. Add the required flavouring and colouring, and pour on to a cold surface, ie a marble slab. As the mixture cools, push the edges to the middle with a buttered knife. Dust with a little icing sugar and pull until the sugar looks dull, taking care not to twist the mixture. Cut into pieces, and leave to stand in a warm place overnight until it is powdery and soft. If the rock is still sticky it means that is has not been pulled enough. Store in an airtight tin.

EDINBURGH, PRINCES STREET 1897 39108

RECIPE

HERRINGS IN OATMEAL

Newhaven fishwives would bring their herrings to sell at the market in Edinburgh, and were famous for their cry 'Caller Herrin!' (Fresh herrings!)

Ingredients:

4 herrings	Pepper
2 tablespoons oatmeal	Fat for frying
Half a teaspoon salt	

Scale and clean the herrings and wash and dry them well. Mix the oatmeal with the salt and pepper and use this to coat the herrings on both sides, pressing the oatmeal well into the herrings. Fry in hot fat for five minutes each side. The herrings can also be grilled if preferred, prepared in the same way, but frying gives more flavour.

QUIZ ANSWERS

1. Edinburgh's elegant architecture has caused it to be referred to as 'The Athens of the North'.

2. In August 1543 two treaties were ratified at Holyrood for the marriage of the infant Mary, Queen of Scots to the English King Henry VIII's son Edward. Scotland at this time was under the governorship of James, 2nd Earl of Arran, a Protestant. He had used bribery, threats and possibly blackmail to persuade the Scottish parliament to agree to the match. However, when all seemed to be arranged, James suddenly had a change of heart and joined the Catholic Mary of Guise (the infant queen's mother) in opposing the wedding. Henry VIII was not impressed and sent an invasion force, which arrived off Newhaven. Edinburgh fell to the troops of the Earl of Hertford, who had Holyrood and the Old Town put to the torch, although the castle was not taken. The episode was referred to as the 'Rough Wooing'.

3. The King's Wall was built in 1450 by order of James II, which separated Edinburgh Castle from the Old Town by the length of a bowshot. This is why the city gate nearest to the castle was named the Upper Bow, and the gate at the bottom of the High Street was called the Netherbow.

4. When the Nor' Loch was drained and new land was available for development, many people were unwilling to move out from the safety of Edinburgh's walls. A reward of £20 was offered to the first person to build a house in the New Town. The first house is still standing in Thistle Court.

EDINBURGH, WAVERLEY BRIDGE FROM PRINCES STREET GARDENS 1883 E24302

5. The novels of Sir Walter Scott made all things Scottish very fashionable. George IV came to Edinburgh in 1822 and attended a ball in full Highland dress, but rather spoiled the effect by wearing pink silk tights.

6. Princes Street is named after the many sons of George III.

7. The Edinburgh writer Robert Louis Stevenson based his successful novel 'Dr Jekyll and Mr Hyde' on the character of Deacon Brodie, who was a respectable town councillor by day and a burglar by night. Brodie lived in what is now Brodie's Close, and was executed in 1788.

8. David Hume.

9. 'The Wealth of Nations' (1776).

10. 'Gardyloo!' - a corrupt form of the French phrase for 'Mind the water!'

THE EDINBURGH
TATTOO AND FESTIVAL

Edinburgh is world-famous for two cultural events which turn the city into a whirl of colour of music, theatre, dance and street entertainment: the Edinburgh International Festival of Music and Drama (and the equally famous Fringe which accompanies it), and the Military Tattoo, both held in late August and early September each year. In 2005, the 200th anniversary of the Battle of Trafalgar, an image of Admiral Nelson was projected on to the castle as a backdrop to the Military Tattoo. Other noteworthy events in Edinburgh's year are the Edinburgh Highland Games, held on the Saturday preceding the festival, and the Royal Scottish Academy Art Exhibition, which is held from late April until early August.

HIGHLAND DANCERS OF NEW ZEALAND AT THE EDINBURGH TATTOO 2005
E24703k (Courtesy of Michael Willcocks)

**ONE OF EDINBURGH'S
STREET ENTERTAINERS 2005**
E24702k (Courtesy of Michael Willcocks)

THE EDINBURGH TATTOO 2005 E24701k (Courtesy of Michael Willcocks)

NEAVES FOOD

NEWINGTON &

23

EDINBURGH, PRINCES STREET, WEST END 1897 39113

FRANCIS FRITH

PIONEER VICTORIAN PHOTOGRAPHER

Francis Frith, founder of the world-famous photographic archive, was a complex and multi-talented man. A devout Quaker and a highly successful Victorian businessman, he was philosophical by nature and pioneering in outlook. By 1855 he had already established a wholesale grocery business in Liverpool, and sold it for the astonishing sum of £200,000, which is the equivalent today of over £15,000,000. Now in his thirties, and captivated by the new science of photography, Frith set out on a series of pioneering journeys up the Nile and to the Near East.

INTRIGUE AND EXPLORATION

He was the first photographer to venture beyond the sixth cataract of the Nile. Africa was still the mysterious 'Dark Continent', and Stanley and Livingstone's historic meeting was a decade into the future. The conditions for picture taking confound belief. He laboured for hours in his wicker dark-room in the sweltering heat of the desert, while the volatile chemicals fizzed dangerously in their trays. Back in London he exhibited his photographs and was 'rapturously cheered' by members of the Royal Society. His reputation as a photographer was made overnight.

VENTURE OF A LIFE-TIME

By the 1870s the railways had threaded their way across the country, and Bank Holidays and half-day Saturdays had been made obligatory by Act of Parliament. All of a sudden the working man and his family were able to enjoy days out, take holidays, and see a little more of the world.

With typical business acumen, Francis Frith foresaw that these new tourists would enjoy having souvenirs to commemorate their days out. For the next thirty years he travelled the country by train and by pony and trap, producing fine photographs of seaside resorts and beauty spots that were keenly bought by millions of Victorians. These prints were painstakingly pasted into family albums and pored over during the dark nights of winter, rekindling precious memories of summer excursions. Frith's studio was soon supplying retail shops all over the country, and by 1890 F Frith & Co had become the greatest specialist photographic publishing company in the world, with over 2,000 sales outlets, and pioneered the picture postcard.

FRANCIS FRITH'S LEGACY

Francis Frith had died in 1898 at his villa in Cannes, his great project still growing. By 1970 the archive he created contained over a third of a million pictures showing 7,000 British towns and villages.

Frith's legacy to us today is of immense significance and value, for the magnificent archive of evocative photographs he created provides a unique record of change in the cities, towns and villages throughout Britain over a century and more. Frith and his fellow studio photographers revisited locations many times down the years to update their views, compiling for us an enthralling and colourful pageant of British life and character.

We are fortunate that Frith was dedicated to recording the minutiae of everyday life. For it is this sheer wealth of visual data, the painstaking chronicle of changes in dress, transport, street layouts, buildings, housing and landscape that captivates us so much today, offering us a powerful link with the past and with the lives of our ancestors.

Computers have now made it possible for Frith's many thousands of images to be accessed almost instantly. The archive offers every one of us an opportunity to examine the places where we and our families have lived and worked down the years. Its images, depicting our shared past, are now bringing pleasure and enlightenment to millions around the world a century and more after his death.

For further information visit: www.francisfrith.com

INTERIOR DECORATION

Frith's photographs can be seen framed and as giant wall murals in thousands of pubs, restaurants, hotels, banks, retail stores and other public buildings throughout Britain. These provide interesting and attractive décor, generating strong local interest and acting as a powerful reminder of gentler days in our increasingly busy and frenetic world.

FRITH PRODUCTS

All Frith photographs are available as prints and posters in a variety of different sizes and styles. In the UK we also offer a range of other gift and stationery products illustrated with Frith photographs, although many of these are not available for delivery outside the UK – see our web site for more information on the products available for delivery in your country.

THE INTERNET

Over 100,000 photographs of Britain can be viewed and purchased on the Frith web site. The web site also includes memories and reminiscences contributed by our customers, who have personal knowledge of localities and of the people and properties depicted in Frith photographs. If you wish to learn more about a specific town or village you may find these reminiscences fascinating to browse. Why not add your own comments if you think they would be of interest to others? See **www.francisfrith.com**

PLEASE HELP US BRING FRITH'S PHOTOGRAPHS TO LIFE

Our authors do their best to recount the history of the places they write about. They give insights into how particular towns and villages developed, they describe the architecture of streets and buildings, and they discuss the lives of famous people who lived there. But however knowledgeable our authors are, the story they tell is necessarily incomplete.

Frith's photographs are so much more than plain historical documents. They are living proofs of the flow of human life down the generations. They show real people at real moments in history; and each of those people is the son or daughter of someone, the brother or sister, aunt or uncle, grandfather or grandmother of someone else. All of them lived, worked and played in the streets depicted in Frith's photographs.

We would be grateful if you would give us your insights into the places shown in our photographs: the streets and buildings, the shops, businesses and industries. Post your memories of life in those streets on the Frith website: what it was like growing up there, who ran the local shop and what shopping was like years ago; if your workplace is shown tell us about your working day and what the building is used for now. Read other visitors' memories and reconnect with your shared local history and heritage. With your help more and more Frith photographs can be brought to life, and vital memories preserved for posterity, and for the benefit of historians in the future.

Wherever possible, we will try to include some of your comments in future editions of our books. Moreover, if you spot errors in dates, titles or other facts, please let us know, because our archive records are not always completely accurate—they rely on 140 years of human endeavour and hand-compiled records. You can email us using the contact form on the website.

Thank you!

For further information, trade, or author enquiries
please contact us at the address below:

**The Francis Frith Collection, Frith's Barn, Teffont,
Salisbury, Wiltshire, England SP3 5QP.**
Tel: +44 (0)1722 716 376 Fax: +44 (0)1722 716 881
e-mail: sales@francisfrith.co.uk **www.francisfrith.com**